Enormous Blue Umbrella

Enormous Blue Umbrella

by Donna Hilbert

MOON
TIDE PRESS

~ 2025 ~

Enormous Blue Umbrella
© Copyright 2025 Donna Hilbert
All rights reserved. No part of this book may be used or reproduced in any manner whatsoever without written permission from either the author or the publisher, except in the case of credited epigraphs or brief quotations embedded in articles or reviews.

Editor-in-chief
Eric Morago

Editor Emeritus
Michael Miller

Marketing/Social Media Specialist
Ellen Webre

Operations Associate
Shelly Holder

Proofreaders
Jeremy Ra

Front cover & interior art
Donna Hilbert

Author photo
Nathaniel Gutman

Book design
Michael Wada

Moon Tide logo design
Abraham Gomez

Enormous Blue Umbrella
is published by Moon Tide Press

Moon Tide Press
6709 Washington Ave. #9297
Whittier, CA 90608
www.moontidepress.com

FIRST EDITION

Printed in the United States of America

ISBN # 978-1-957799-27-8

for my beloved family
for Nathaniel
for my workshop
for Jill Young who has read every word
for Torey Eden, forever

Contents

I

Passage at Nineteen	14
Enormous Blue Umbrella	15
Iron Skillet	16
Field Notes: The Woods in April	17
Chocolate Milk	18
I Bite My Tongue	19
Walking Door County on Palm Sunday	20
Walk Before Sun-up, August	21
The Stapler Speaks	22
Shade	23

II

Iris in the Mind	26
New	27
What the Walk is Like	28
What Birds	29
Ode to Purple	30
Field Notes: The Woods in May	31
The Deer	32
After Illness	33
One Day Past Labor Day, I Walk the Beach	34
Thursday, Dave, the Bay	35
Ineffable	36
Opening	37

III

Spiritus	40
Walk Before Coffee, After a Glance at the Times	41
Encounter at Gelson's	42
The Kreutzer Sonata	43
Tolstoy's Kreutzer	44
Field Notes: Peninsula in January	45
Flaw	46
Ardea Herodias	47
Wordle 453	48
Back Deck, Morning	49
Low Tide	50
The Wait	51

IV

The Phone	54
Grace	55
I Visit the Dentist	56
Walking my Dog in the Dark	57
I Do 100 Flying Cloud Hands While the Coffee Drips	58
Summer	59
Neocona Crucifera	60
One Last Trip with Mother	61
Because We Grieve	62
Mourning Doves	63
This Boat	64
Tongues	65

V

Arms	68
After the Birds Begin to Sing from the Trees	69
Good Start	70
Field Notes: Peninsula Spring	71
Reading Zagajewski	72
What I Would Miss	73
Bad Weather	74
Ribollita	75
Thank You Note	76
More	77
About the Author	80
Acknowledgements	81

. . . this most excellent canopy, the air, look you, this brave o'erhanging firmament, this majestical roof fretted with golden fire . . .

—William Shakespeare

Solvitur Ambulando It is solved by walking.

— Diogenes

What cannot be said will be wept.

— Sappho

Now is made out of ghosts.

— William Stafford

And is not the lute that soothes your spirit the very wood that was hollowed with knives

— Kahil Gabrin

I

Passage at Nineteen

I hold you to my breast
for the slow ride home
through falling snow.
Flesh of my flesh,
I am reborn, dancing
in terror and joy
balanced on the eyelash
of a blinking god.

Enormous Blue Umbrella

Enormous, sad, and blue, this umbrella
we walk beneath. It's winter still,
but who could tell with sky so poignant
blue it stings the eye, and merely a tinge
of cold informs the air. Passersby don't
seem to notice the mountain's sharp
outline beyond the bayside homes.

And across the boulevard, across the sand,
beyond the stranded ships, Catalina shines
like tin foil. It's the walkers I wonder about:
sad faces, our caps pulled down, moving fast,
no place special to go, so fierce to get there.

Iron Skillet

I'm cleaning you now
with coarse salt and a paper towel.
Skillet of my mother, grandmother,
and her mother before her.
You've fried chickens
raised, killed, plucked, dressed
on farms, in backyards
by generations of women whose children
watched in fascination and fear.
You've fried bacon, eggs over easy,
baked cornbread, baked biscuits, grilled
sandwiches, fried fold-over pies for
farmers, mechanics, civil servants, teachers.

Last night, I blackened a sea bass
on your flat belly where tonight,
potatoes and carrots will nestle and roast
while an omelet browns on top of the stove.
Skillet, trusty instrument of nurture,
I praise your amazing utility, plurality
of purpose, example of endurance.
How easily you fashion meal after meal,
serve us, feed us, re-season, restore.

Field Notes: The Woods in April

Night animal cries are different here,
and grievance dreams invade my sleep.
*

Cardinal sings *I pity you, I pity you.*
My dear red bird, I'm not that sad.
*

I watch four deer watching me,
a pane of glass between us.
*

Good Friday, Passover, in midst of Ramadan,
first robins, a mist of snow.
*

I walk the path the deer walk,
pine needles umber on the woodland floor.
*

Chocolate Milk

That day I feared
I'd never stop crying,
my tears a torrent
taking me out to sea,
Dr. Helene asked what soothed me
as a sad, and scared, small kid.
Chocolate milk, I said.
Drink that, she said.
Drink until you stop the crying.

I drove through the drive-in dairy,
bought a can of chocolate syrup
and a gallon of milk,
and drank, and drank, and drank,
until my life was sweet
enough to greet my children
skipping through the door from school.

I Bite My Tongue

I'm at Gelson's bakery counter
when *Fly Me to the Moon*
comes over the sound system
and I make a face and say
something rude, like "puke."

The clerk, who doesn't look
old enough to know the tune
or hold a job, says,
"You don't like this song?"

"Not the song," I tell her, "It's *him*."
I gather steam, feel my face flush.

I rush on. "I saw him once.
He muffed his famous songs,
even with cue cards. His son
was on the piano. He cursed him,
called him stupid."

The girl's face melts from quizzical
to sad. She slips my bagels into a bag,
and says, "I don't want to feel
bad things about families."

I return my sword to its sheath.
Clamp my teeth. Hard.

Walking Door County on Palm Sunday

I'm from L.A., so I welcome the way
drivers wave with their whole hand
in greeting, when they pass me walking
the highway leading, I'm told, to Green Bay.
I imagine they smile and say *good day*
on their way to the church I am walking
away from, white church with a steeple
I, bad navigator, use for my still point
to find the path back to my temporary home.

I fear the sun won't hold.
At the bend in the road, I turn toward the steeple.
Then, I turn again and head back to the bay.
Though uphill and hard, the way home
is always faster, and I can walk it in the rain.

Walk Before Sun-up, August

Anthuriums abloom
in a neighbor's yard,

take me back to Christmas
in the old house,

that year we abandoned
tree and tinsel

to cheer ourselves instead

with bouquets
of crimson bracts,

golden-tongued
open mouths of joy.

The Stapler Speaks

I'm not made for licking
or fondling, so don't complain
I'm cold and taste of nothing.
What I do, I do well—
fastening together what might be thrust
asunder by the smallest gust
or the brisk touch
of a careless fist.

You can see your face
on my slick surface, check
your lipstick, look
for that sniglet of kale stuck
in the crevice, between
your front two teeth.
If it's pain you're after, slip
one finger between my teeth
and push.

Shade

I'm looking for lipstick
the shade, exact match
of my mimi's lips,
whose color never faded
from illness, from age.
At the end, still peach,
still full, still sweet
as summer fruit.

II

Iris in the Mind

I so anticipate the iris bloom
I think I see one from the window
of the room where I sit, writing.

I go outside to check and find
only reflection on a rock.

The iris will rise and fall
in its own time, and I settle
for the iris in my mind.

New

That time in the park
at the end of the street

our dogs off leash
and we are off leash too

our love so new
we kiss and kiss

not caring for once
who sees us

what might be said
or be construed.

What the Walk is Like

A narrow path through the valley
fire barreling down the hill

whether to run through the flames
or turn, run, out-run, or not

slip from the path to the chasm
call out from the smoky deep

fear in sleep, dream in grief

What Birds

What birds are these inky V's
against the morning sky?
I wish my camera were nearby
to capture their grand flight,
but no, just my paltry sight.

I am dismayed to look away
with only memory's faulty room
to hold the marvel I see, and love,
but cannot praise by name.

Ode to Purple

O how I love you, purple pen
given to me by Shannon, my friend:
fountain pen, sitting so prettily
between finger and thumb,
and within your chamber

mélange of red blood and blue
taking me straight to Big Hair
and purple skirts so long they graze
the top of my boots, and I shun undies
to be gleefully naughty in public.

And back to the purple sweater
bought for yearbook photos,
ninth grade, at Orbach's LA
taking a bus from the West Valley
with savvy, smart, Ann from New York,

and further back to Mom,
who when re-doing my room,
refused my vision of purple walls—
excluding lavender, lilac, puce, no matter
my pleas, no matter my howls.

O eggplant, O plum, O yard full of iris,
O purple beanie crocheted by Aruni
O overblown phrases, and broken
and bruised, beating hearts.
Bring it all on! Because I swear

by the goddess of excess and beauty,
I freaking love you, Purple.

Field Notes: The Woods in May

Against gray rock   red tulip rises
*
Spring unfurls   one flower at a time
*
Sunrise on forsythia   dazzle of gold
*
At the bay   inhalation of Mayflies
*
Jonquil   orange kiss inside the white
*
On a bed of leaves   doe round with life
*

The Deer

The deer don't dine on daffodils,
or so I'm told. I'd like to think
they love the plucky beauties
as I do—admire, desire,
but choose to leave in peace
their yellow grace
and eat instead a duller
springtime hue.

After Illness

After illness, I awaken remembering that I love my life,
and enter the garden to water,
though clouds are darkening and the forecast calls for rain.

I turn the hose on spindly fennel, tamping down the middle
until its licorice breath releases
and I remember that I love my life.

Water beads on shafts of rosemary, growing even in my garden,
though righteousness I once could claim has long been leached away.
Clouds are darkening and the forecast calls for rain.

I crave the taste of lavender growing fragrant
in my garden and on my tongue blooms *Fern Leaf,*
French, Sachet. I awaken to remembering that I love my life.

Honeysuckle, Morning Glory, Bougainvillea
tangle to an arbor making shelter in my garden
should darkening clouds unloose the forecast rain.

Mockingbirds, unimpressed by human pain,
still gather in my garden. I hear their song
and I remember that I love my life,
though clouds are darkening and the forecast calls for rain.

One Day Past Labor Day, I Walk the Beach

In the realm of totalitarian kitsch, all answers are given in advance and preclude any questions.

— Milan Kundera, *The Unbearable Lightness of Being*

Which do you prefer: water bottles, beer bottles, cans,
abandoned sandals in the sand, or kitsch
adorning mansionettes with starred and striped
pinwheels spinning among plastic-pink flamingos,
and door-way blocking blow-up Uncle Sams?

Trash will be picked up. Laborers will return to labor.
Kitsch will beget more kitsch: righteous, cheerful, smug.

Thursday, Dave, the Bay

I hear "76 Trombones" coming up
behind me and know it's Dave
with his little dog and a bag of scones
from a nearby bakery.
Dave turns his tinny transistor off,
and says, "I'm sorry," showing me
his empty bag. "Late for my walk," I say.
"Next Thursday," Dave says, marching on.

I go back to watching two green herons
perched on neighboring boats,
facing one another, still as stone.

Ineffable

Something about the stack
of kayaks on bay-side sand

red, green, blue,
and sunrise dropping gold

on the whole tableau:
the boats, the sand, the water below.

Opening

They capture light, my neighbor says
of his many angled windows
fronting water on the bay side's shore.

Who wouldn't want to capture light
the way a child traps fireflies
on a summer night?

In the waning dark, I catch what I can
with my cell phone's eager eye,
and greet again the great window opening.

III

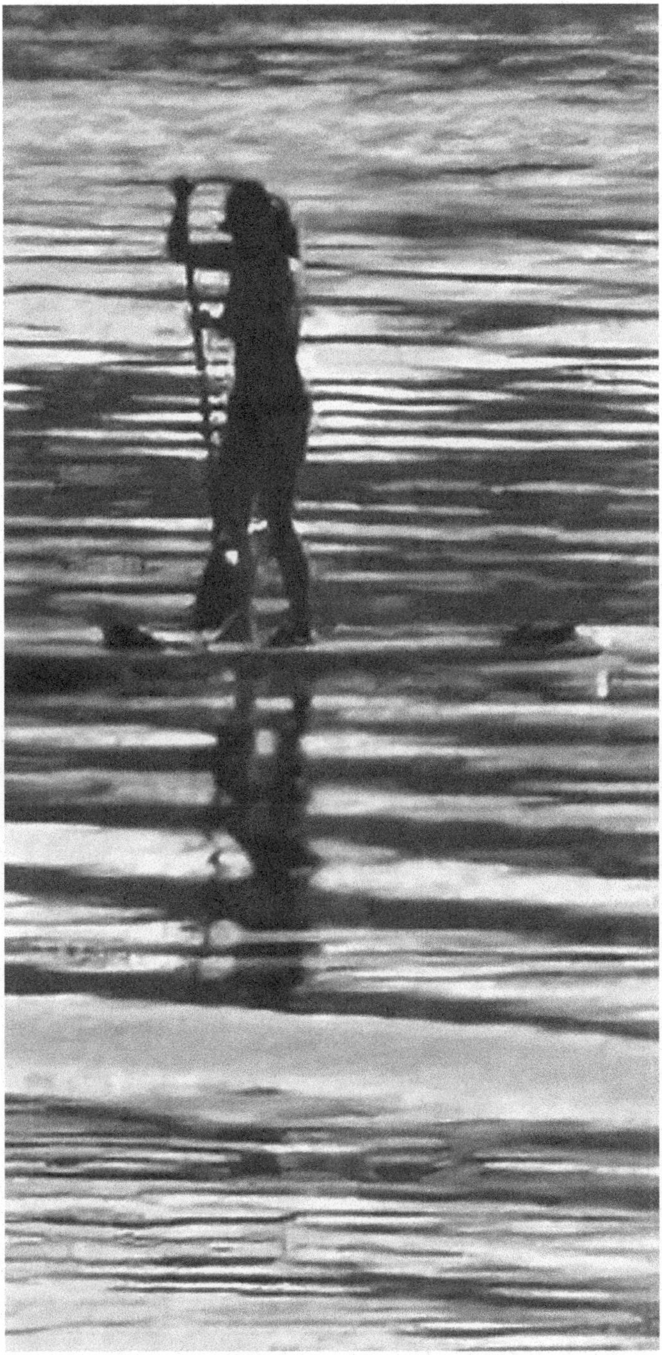

Spiritus

I waken to the sound of breathing
so loud I think it's you beside me.
But no, love, it's me. My breath, alone.

Walk Before Coffee, After a Glance at the *Times*

I say good morning to a passerby
but hear, instead, good *mourning*
in my head, and I am dazed
by the ambiguity of homophones.

And, on the turntable of my brain
spins a melody I hum, but can't abide:
Morning has broken. No. Morning
is broken. In present tense, it sings.

Encounter at Gelson's

On the first day we feel safe
touching another human being
outside of our tiny family pod,
I see a woman from my neighborhood
embrace a favorite box-boy. The kid
is on the spectrum, and super good
at his job. The hug is long. They pull back,
look at one another, hug again.

I kill time by the shopping cart carrel
to take in the scene, blow my nose
into an old mask, dab at my eyes
with my sleeve. I don't want to be seen
bawling my head off at Gelson's
fancy, prepared food counter.

The Kreutzer Sonata

The Kreutzer Sonata
is perfect for cooking:
about forty minutes
adagio through presto.
The insistent opening ideal
for mincing garlic and onion.
Forty minutes for risotto
from impulse to finish.

Forty minutes at 425 to oven-roast
potatoes and fish in a cast-iron skillet
(after 20 minutes, slip fish into the pan
with potatoes, and make a green salad).

Forty minutes to start
a good soup on the stove.
Put the soup on to simmer,
and begin the sonata again.

Tolstoy's Kreutzer

> *... art takes up what life has censored.*
>
> — Agnes Callard

Tolstoy's sonata takes place on a train,
and is, of course, a story
of passion, debauchery, jealousy, death.
What is it in travel that tenders confession?
A penitent whose confessor
can't manage escape?

En route, Pozdnyshev gives voice
to the screech of his demons: a leitmotif
of Tolstoy's loathing the tethers of flesh.
O what sad uses sublime music is blamed for!
Of the *Immortal Beloved,* we know precious little.
For this I'm joyfully, eternally glad.

Field Notes: Peninsula in January

A foretaste of spring   on waterfowl wings
*
Heron builds a nest in the lone coral tree   others in palm after palm.
*
Three days of sun   a tsunami warning   a bit of rain.
*
The sky returns to mottled gray   just one day
*
Then angled light   dry and bright.
*

Flaw

I dreamt I spoilt my quilt
to not offend the gods.

I am not a quilter,
and perfection not my lot.

Ardea Herodias

Heron doesn't quarrel with the world.
He sits atop the powerlines, keeps still, keeps slight,

until some sound, or sign, unknowable to humankind
unfolds his ancient wings to re-enact the origin of flight.

Wordle 453

I begin with *angst*
continue to *drift*
arrive at *doubt*

Back Deck, Morning

On the lattice ceiling
dew drops cling

to nail heads strung
like lightning bugs

as if to catch
the morning sun.

With a glint of magic
the day has begun.

Low Tide

I love the way the water pulls
the shoreline back
showing what lies beneath:

old stairway
next to the dock, a few steps
laced with barnacles and moss,

another pathway into the mystery.

The Wait

I waken to your hand
holding mine,
you, on the floor by the bed,
the morning after I said
we are through.

Your tender vigil coaxed
the buds of love to sprout again
after the dormant season,
when I had ceased belief
in anything but grief.

IV

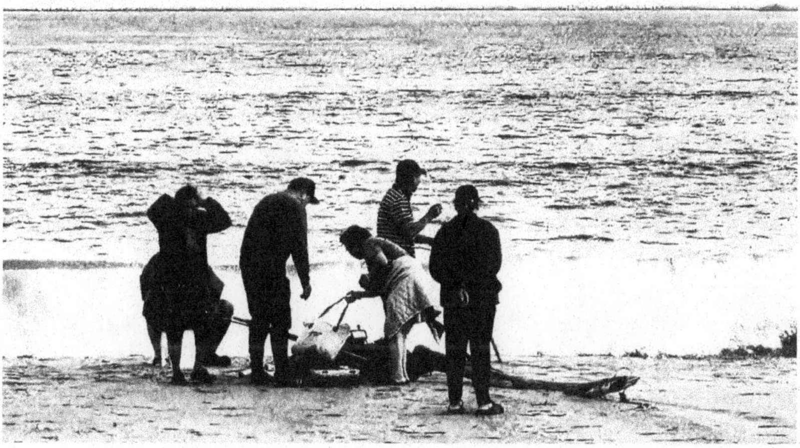

The Phone

"There are two types of reactors,"
my grad-school-psych professor said,
"when hearing the phone, one says
yay who's calling me! The other says
shit who's bothering me." But I say
there are three. The third is me.
I say, who's dead?

Grace
after Ellen Rowland's No Small Thing

It's no small grace
preparing the coffee pot,
then stepping out
in morning dark

to stand beneath a palm,
and listen
for osprey's
high-pitched song,

then return in rising sun
to coffee, hot, to fill
the waiting cup, and drink.

It's no small grace
to brace one's self
with simple pleasure

before the day goes wrong.

I Visit the Dentist

Dr. R will fill the divot,
buff the edges
until smooth,
until my tongue
forgets the damage
from my zealous brush.
Upper Buccal, Surface Posterior

I wish Dr. R could buff
the rough edges off
my demeanor,
or at least smooth the corners
of my kitchen counters,
where I often gouge
the dorsal side of my hands,
arms flailing in anger,
desperation,
and sometimes, joy.

Walking my Dog in the Dark

Natasha, my pup, knows how to wake up
to the world: Look
how she stands on hind legs,
paws on the sea-wall, to watch
a guy on the beach toss a football
into the air and catch it, again, and again,
amusing himself as day begins.

I snap a shot or two with my phone
of the ball's rise and decline.
When the sun pops up, my pup and I walk on.

I Do 100 Flying Cloud Hands While the Coffee Drips

In a copper-bottomed pot, my mother perked coffee,
adding a pinch of salt to bring out the flavor.
I was a kid and I thought it was good
with lots of milk and a little sugar.

Later, she adopted Coffee Mate: You can't tell the difference!
Then Cool Whip: Just as good as Whipped Cream!
Some new margarine: As yummy as butter, maybe better!

When I eschewed meat, she declared I couldn't possibly taste
the chicken broth base in the casserole, or the bacon fat
seasoning green beans. Oh, how she wished me to swallow
what gagged me, then open my mouth and drip praise.

Summer
for T.E.

Solstice again. One year, we waded into the sea
to wash crystals. (It was all about *feng shui*.)
The water was cold, the sky, cloud gray.

Back in the house, you fingered your name
onto the foggy windows, with hearts for O's,
frames, and punctuation.

I took a photo of this.
Now, it's proof you were here,
and for a time, happy.

Neocona Crucifera

She poses in full red-spotted splendor
neocona crucifera, orb weaver,
her black eyes meeting mine.

O many-legged beauty,
are you watching me watch you?

One Last Trip with Mother

My mother twists long tendrils
of my hair into pin curls,
opening bobby pins with her teeth,
fastening the fat rounds to my scalp.

She laughs when I say *"ouch!"*
as I had done eons ago, when I was a girl.
This time, I laugh too, daughter again
surrendering my head to her rough fingers,
and her tender ministrations.

Because We Grieve

Because we grieve,
I hold you close.
And, from another plane
a current enters us both,
grown women
who need a mother,
who need a daughter.

We are fastened now,
until we don't know
whose heart is beating
in which body,
or who is breathing,
or what god to thank
for hurtling this bolt
shocking us back
into our altered selves.

Mourning Doves

Because the potted plant
on the back porch needs water,
I come nose to beak
with a brooding dove;
too late to stop the water
pouring from my pitcher,
I flood the nest.

Her mate watches from powerlines.
She moves to a nearby ledge,
leaving the egg alone in the sodden pot.

Throughout the day, I go outside
 and see the doves maintaining vigil.

By nightfall, the pair is gone.
I peer into the pot.
Nothing remains of nest or feather.
Not a trace of shell.

This Boat
for T.E.

Were you two or three?
Strapped to my lap in the kayak
I paddled into the wetlands
past the sign that read "Go Back."

Herons, pelicans, cormorants
flew close enough to touch,
and sun dazzled the murk below.

"In this boat, we can go anywhere,"
you said, then pressed your cheek
to my breast, and slept.

You were almost grown,
when you chose the unknown water.
If there were signs ahead,
I failed to heed, or even see, them.

Tongues

I gouged my tongue
on the cruel edge of a carrot.
Yes, it bled.

I did not swallow the fly
that drowned in my coffee,
though it rested on my tongue
until I realized it was not a crumb,
but a creature, dead.

My nose did not break
when I dropped my phone
onto its bridge while reading
news from the war zone
in my safe, but troubled, bed.

Who could find sleep
while naming the dead?

V

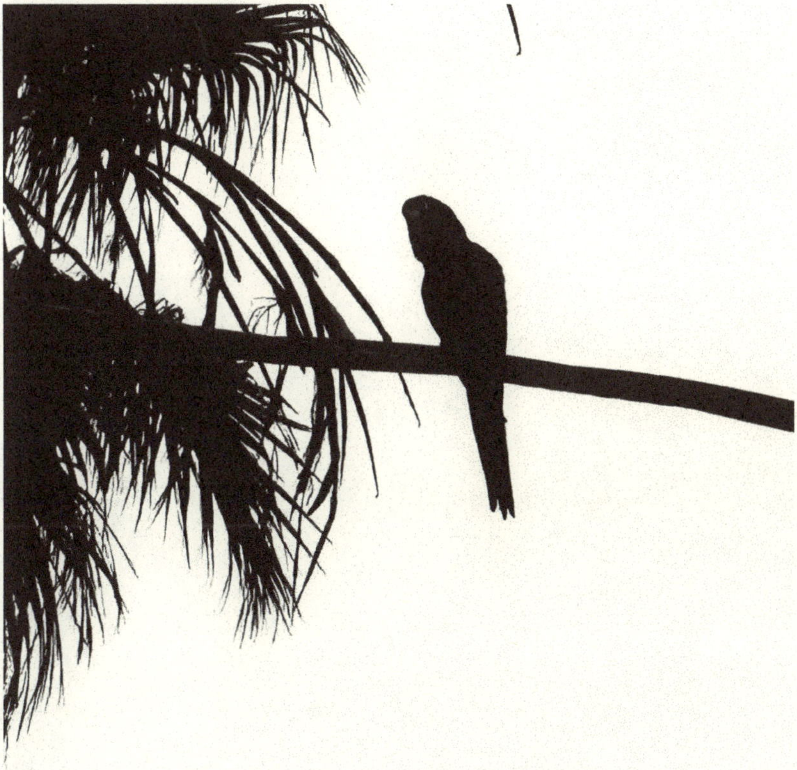

Arms

Cracked branch of a white ash
leans into the Japanese cherry.

Even trees need friendly arms
to hold them.

After the Birds Begin to Sing from the Trees

Before the sun makes its way over the bay
before the sky softens to gray
before the blaze of day begins

I rise, pull on my jeans, lace up my shoes
and enter the day, before the neighbors
are out, before the traffic begins,

before the phone rings,
while the day is blank as a page,
before I pick up my pen,

thank you, I say, let this day begin.

Good Start

A good start to a regular day,
is pulling into Gelson's parking lot,
when the store opens at seven.
"It's my favorite time, too,"
the young clerk says,
"because this early, nobody's mad."

Muffins are fresh and warm
from the oven, shelves neat, laden
with promise, produce glistens
like straight from the garden,
and for once—Hallelujah—
there's a bin of organic potatoes,
and nary a spud sprouts an eye!

Field Notes: Peninsula Spring

First day of spring,
the air is cold, the sky is drear,
but by his presence on this pier
egret claims that spring is here.

Wind and rain slap at my face
speak a different time and place
no room for spring's expected grace
with winter's grip so tight, so dear.

Second day of spring, big wind, big rain,
ground's a sump not fit to tromp in
seagulls madly flap for purchase
in this swamp, this swirl.

Reading Zagajewski

This copper pen,
my beloved's fine gift,
reclines in the spine
of the book I am living
again, marking my place
between "Reading Milosz"
and "Walk Through This Town."

Pen, two weeks in the web
made by finger and thumb,
its patina flames like music
alive in the mind,
like the poet himself,
outliving himself, and Natasha,
my dog, rests her head
on my feet while I read.

What I Would Miss

What I would miss most
are moments like this:

favorite pen in my hand
gliding the page

as if the pen were a skater
on a rink made of paper,

morning coffee
hot shock on my tongue.

Bad Weather

I have been the fallen bird
waiting for the ride

that never came, walking
home in beating rain.

I have been the forlorn traveler,
familiar in the corridors

of waiting.
I have been the fallen bird

pulled out of grief's bad weather,
caressed and held together,

spoon fed until I wished
to die, then live, again.

Ribollita

I praise the way you save
stale bread left on the shelf too long,
rinds of Parmesan tough to grate,
old greens not crisp enough
for salad, but fine for soup
re-boiled from what's on hand.

I love the way you salvage
bruised tomato, sprouting onion,
imperfect squash, laying no morsel
to mold, nothing to waste,
filling each space with aroma
of soup, saying supper, *mangia!*
come eat, come safely, come home.

Thank You Note

Dearest,

Thank you for staying up all night,
setting an alarm for every three hours
making sure I get my meds on time
to stay ahead of pain.

You straighten the sheets.
You coax me to eat.
You bring croissants,
and the only yogurt
I can stomach.

You let me cry without comment,
though I know it pains you
to see me suffer.

You stand by while I shower,
adjust temperature and force
to not unthread
the hidden sutures.

Note, Dearest, I will do this for you.
You, who appeared from the blue
and gave me the future.

More

I want more pages in my day planner
with its tidy squares and room on the side
for "to dos" to be checked off, and I want
that list to never end. I want one page
after another and another to appear
in unending supply, the way peanut
butter jars appear in the cupboard and I'm
aghast at their number, and know you've
been to that big box store once again,
so, it takes me forever to find the tiny
jar of saffron stuck in the back.
I want more dreams of falling
for the joyful relief at awakening
from the chasm of sleep to consult
my day planner and tick off tasks
that annoy me. I want more days
to gripe in my mind about tiny hillocks
of crumbs, you've left on the counter
while slicing bread from Gusto's
on Fourth Street, bought in such quantity
and stuffed in the freezer, that I can't find
my tiny pint of mint chip ice cream.
Then the drip drop of red wine, the drip drop
of tomato from the salad you made
for me last night—I want more of that
on the counter. I want more mornings
when your heavy breathing wakens
me from sleep, when your five-pillow chateau
threatens to topple and smother me,
and I get up with the sun and head
out for my walk when the glorious
unfolding of the day is waiting.

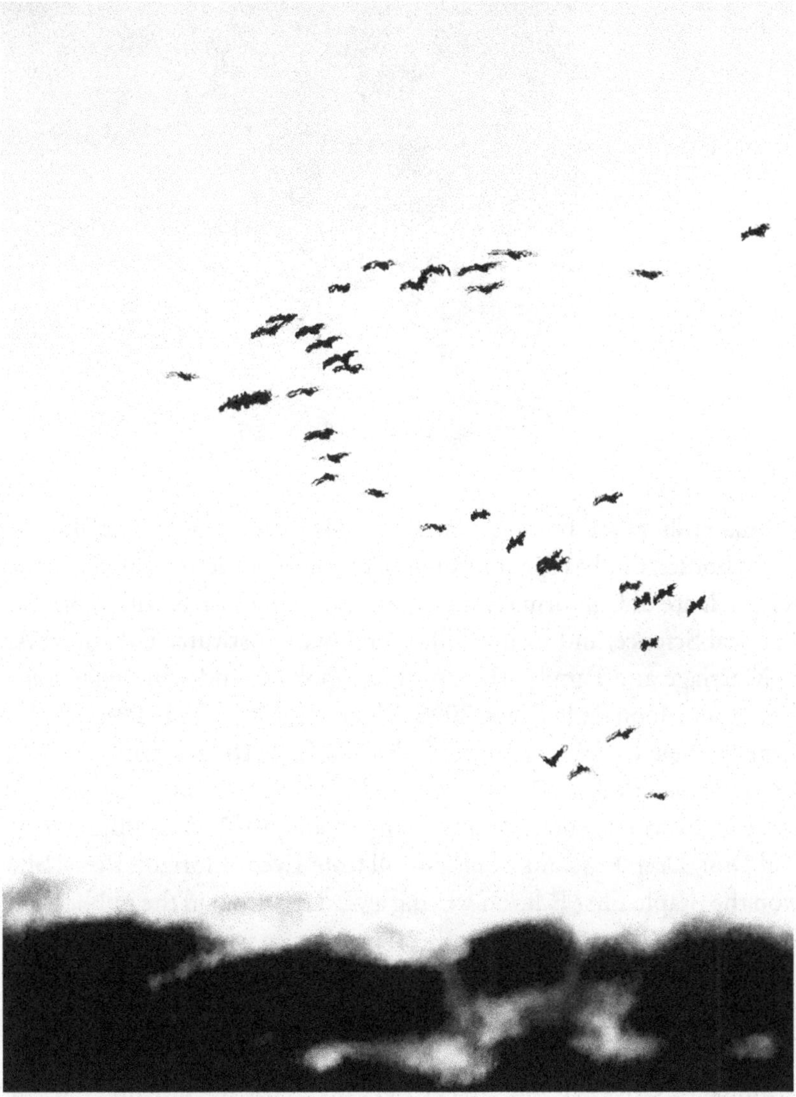

About the Author

Donna Hilbert was born in Grandfield, Oklahoma near the Oklahoma-Texas border, but has spent most of her life in Southern California. She is a graduate of California State University, Long Beach, with a B.A. in Political Science, and from Phillips Graduate Institute, with an M.A. in Marriage and Family Therapy. Her books include *Enormous Blue Umbrella*, Moon Tide Press, 2025, *Threnody*, Moon Tide Press, 2022, *Gravity: New & Selected Poems*, Tebot Bach, 2018, *The Green Season*, World Parade Books, 2009, *Traveler in Paradise: New and Selected Poems*, PEARL Editions, 2004; *Transforming Matter*, PEARL 2000; *Feathers and Dust*, *Deep Red*, and *Mansions*, all from Event Horizon Press. She won the Staple First Edition writing award resulting in the publication in England of the short story collection, *Women who Make Money and the Men Who Love Them*. Her work is the subject of the short film *Grief Becomes Me*, by director Christine Fugate, which was shown as a work-in-progress at the Kentucky Women Writers Conference and is included in *Grief Becomes Me: A Love Story*, the documentary about her life and work. She writes and teaches private workshops in Long Beach, California, where she makes her home.

Acknowledgements

I thank Jerod Santek and the staff and board of Write On Door County for the generous residencies during which many of the poems in *Enormous Blue Umbrella* were written. I also thank the gracious editors of the following journals and anthologies where poems in *Enormous Blue Umbrella* first appeared, sometimes with slightly different form or title.

Journals
Beach Chair Press: Field Notes: Peninsula Spring, What Birds

Chiron Review: One Day Past Labor Day I Walk the Beach

Eclectica: Reading Zagajewski

First Literary Review East: Arms, Wordle 453

Journal of Radical Wonder: Ode to my Purple Pen, *Ardea Herodias*, Walking my Dog in the Dark, Because We Grieve, Iris in the Mind, One Last Trip with Mother, I Visit the Dentist,
Field Notes: The Woods in May

ONE ART: Ribollita, Enormous Blue Umbrella, Iron Skillet, *Spiritus*, The Kreutzer Sonata, Walk Before Coffee After a Glance at The Times, I Do 100 Flying Cloud Hands While the Coffee Drips, Anthurium in August, Passage at Nineteen, Opening, More, The Wait, The Phone, Bad Weather, Summer, Shade, Low Tide, Encounter in Gelson's, Thursday, Dave the Bay, Tongues, Mourning Doves, Good Start, Chocolate Milk, This Boat, New

Sheila-Na-Gig: Field Notes: Peninsula in January, Walking Door County on Palm Sunday, Field Notes: The Woods in April, After the Birds Begin to Sing from the Trees, Back Deck Morning, Neocona Crucifera, Grace

Your Daily Poem: Iron Skillet

Verse Virtual: Iron Skillet, The Kreutzer Sonata, Walking my Dog in the Dark, Enormous Blue Umbrella, More, Walk Before Coffee After a Glance at the Times, Iris in my Mind, Field Notes: The Woods in May, Summer, Shade, Ribollita

Anthologies
Poetry of Presence II: Ribollita

The Wonder of Small Things: Ribollita

Ovation: Tongues

Love: The Wait

Also Available from Moon Tide Press

Sky Leaning Toward Winter, Terri Niccum (2024)
Living the Sundown: A Caregiving Memoir,
    G. Murray Thomas (2024)
Figure Study, Kathryn de Lancellotti (2024)
Suffer for This: Love, Sex, Marriage, & Rock 'N' Roll,
    Victor D. Infante (2024)
What Blooms in the Dark, Emily J. Mundy (2024)
Fable, Bryn Wickerd (2024)
Diamond Bars 2, David A. Romero (2024)
Safe Handling, Rebecca Evans (2024)
More Jerkumstances: New & Selected Poems, Barbara Eknoian (2024)
Dissection Day, Ally McGregor (2023)
He's a Color Until He's Not, Christian Hanz Lozada (2023)
The Language of Fractions, Nicelle Davis (2023)
Paradise Anonymous, Oriana Ivy (2023)
Now You Are a Missing Person, Susan Hayden (2023)
Maze Mouth, Brian Sonia-Wallace (2023)
Tangled by Blood, Rebecca Evans (2023)
Another Way of Loving Death, Jeremy Ra (2023)
Kissing the Wound, J.D. Isip (2023)
Feed It to the River, Terhi K. Cherry (2022)
*Beat Not Beat: An Anthology of California Poets Screwing
    on the Beat and Post-Beat Tradition* (2022)
*When There Are Nine: Poems Celebrating the Life and Achievements
    of Ruth Bader Ginsburg* (2022)
The Knife Thrower's Daughter, Terri Niccum (2022)
2 Revere Place, Aruni Wijesinghe (2022)
Here Go the Knives, Kelsey Bryan-Zwick (2022)
Trumpets in the Sky, Jerry Garcia (2022)
Threnody, Donna Hilbert (2022)
A Burning Lake of Paper Suns, Ellen Webre (2021)
Instructions for an Animal Body, Kelly Gray (2021)
Head *V* Heart: New & Selected Poems, Rob Sturma (2021)

Sh!t Men Say to Me: A Poetry Anthology in Response to Toxic Masculinity (2021)
Flower Grand First, Gustavo Hernandez (2021)
Everything is Radiant Between the Hates, Rich Ferguson (2020)
When the Pain Starts: Poetry as Sequential Art, Alan Passman (2020)
This Place Could Be Haunted If I Didn't Believe in Love, Lincoln McElwee (2020)
Impossible Thirst, Kathryn de Lancellotti (2020)
Lullabies for End Times, Jennifer Bradpiece (2020)
Crabgrass World, Robin Axworthy (2020)
Contortionist Tongue, Dania Ayah Alkhouli (2020)
The only thing that makes sense is to grow, Scott Ferry (2020)
Dead Letter Box, Terri Niccum (2019)
Tea and Subtitles: Selected Poems 1999-2019, Michael Miller (2019)
At the Table of the Unknown, Alexandra Umlas (2019)
The Book of Rabbits, Vince Trimboli (2019)
Everything I Write Is a Love Song to the World, David McIntire (2019)
Letters to the Leader, HanaLena Fennel (2019)
Darwin's Garden, Lee Rossi (2019)
Dark Ink: A Poetry Anthology Inspired by Horror (2018)
Drop and Dazzle, Peggy Dobreer (2018)
Junkie Wife, Alexis Rhone Fancher (2018)
The Moon, My Lover, My Mother, & the Dog, Daniel McGinn (2018)
Lullaby of Teeth: An Anthology of Southern California Poetry (2017)
Angels in Seven, Michael Miller (2016)
A Likely Story, Robbi Nester (2014)
Embers on the Stairs, Ruth Bavetta (2014)
The Green of Sunset, John Brantingham (2013)
The Savagery of Bone, Timothy Matthew Perez (2013)
The Silence of Doorways, Sharon Venezio (2013)
Cosmos: An Anthology of Southern California Poetry (2012)
Straws and Shadows, Irena Praitis (2012)
In the Lake of Your Bones, Peggy Dobreer (2012)
I Was Building Up to Something, Susan Davis (2011)

Hopeless Cases, Michael Kramer (2011)
One World, Gail Newman (2011)
What We Ache For, Eric Morago (2010)
Now and Then, Lee Mallory (2009)
Pop Art: An Anthology of Southern California Poetry (2009)
In the Heaven of Never Before, Carine Topal (2008)
A Wild Region, Kate Buckley (2008)
Carving in Bone: An Anthology of Orange County Poetry (2007)
Kindness from a Dark God, Ben Trigg (2007)
A Thin Strand of Lights, Ricki Mandeville (2006)
Sleepyhead Assassins, Mindy Nettifee (2006)
Tide Pools: An Anthology of Orange County Poetry (2006)
Lost American Nights: Lyrics & Poems, Michael Ubaldini (2006)

Patrons

Moon Tide Press would like to thank the following people for their support in helping publish the finest poetry from the Southern California region. To sign up as a patron, visit www.moontidepress.com or send an email to publisher@moontidepress.com.

Anonymous
Robin Axworthy
Conner Brenner
Nicole Connolly
Bill Cushing
Susan Davis
Kristen Baum DeBeasi
Peggy Dobreer
Kate Gale
Dennis Gowans
Alexis Rhone Fancher
HanaLena Fennel
Half Off Books & Brad T. Cox
Donna Hilbert
Jim & Vicky Hoggatt
Michael Kramer
Ron Koertge & Bianca Richards
Gary Jacobelly
Ray & Christi Lacoste

Jeffery Lewis
Zachary & Tammy Locklin
Lincoln McElwee
David McIntire
José Enrique Medina
Michael Miller &
Rachanee Srisavasdi
Michelle & Robert Miller
Ronny & Richard Morago
Terri Niccum
Andrew November
Jeremy Ra
Luke & Mia Salazar
Jennifer Smith
Roger Sponder
Andrew Turner
Rex Wilder
Mariano Zaro
Wes Bryan Zwick